LINKEDIN SKILL ASSESSMENTS TEST PYTHON PROGRAMMING QUESTIONS FOR PRACTICE - TECHNICAL SKILLS QUIZZES

LINKEDIN SKILL ASSESSMENT SERIES: PYTHON GUIDE FOR MULTIPLE CHOICE TESTS MCQS

AV EDITORIAL BOARD

ISBN 979-888521581-7

Contents

CHAPTER I

LinkedIn Skill Assessments Tests

Q. What is LinkedIn Skill Assessments?
A. LinkedIn Skill Assessments is a feature that allows LinkedIn members to take assessments on various skills to test and demonstrate their knowledge of the skills by completing assessments specific to those skills and showcasing their proficiency in those skills on their profile. These assessments are categorized as technical, business, and design skills. You can take an assessment on your mobile device but it is recommend to take them using your laptop or desktop computer.

Q. What does an assessment consist of?
A. A typical assessment consists of 15 multiple choice questions and each question tests at least one concept or subskill. The questions are timed and must be completed in one session. On average you have 1.5 minutes to complete each question and each test must be taken in one sitting. Most of the Skill Assessments also provide a couple of sample questions. To take an assessment, all you have to do is navigate to the skills section of your profile and select the relevant Skill Assessment. If you have a disability, you can activate the accessibility for the Skill Assessment feature. This will allow you additional time to complete each question.

Q. How is the quality of an assessment maintained?
A. LinkedIn Skill Assessments are produced by subject matter experts and leaders in the LinkedIn Learning community, who have extensive experience in generating exam and certification content. To improve the quality and relevancy of assessments:
Multiple writers, instructors, and authors write the questions.
Peer reviewers regularly provide feedback to improve the content.
Each question is timed, which makes it difficult to look up answers while taking the skill assessment.
A computer-based methodology called adaptive testing is used to recognize your skill level and then adjust the questions you're asked accordingly.

Q. When will we get results of the Assessments?
A. Once you've completed an assessment, your answers will be scored, and an assessment report will be generated. You can view it at any time from the Skills page, under the Results tab. Your score is private by default, meaning that you can control the visibility of the results. If you score in the top 30% (determined by comparing your score against a curated benchmark), you'll receive a skill badge, which you can opt to display on your profile and in recruiter searches.

Q. What is a skill badge?
A. A skill badge:
Represents that you've taken a Skill Assessment and demonstrated that you are highly skilled in that area.
Signals to other members and recruiters that you've taken the initiative to show your skill proficiency. This can help you form beneficial relationships and help to surface more relevant content or opportunities for you on LinkedIn.
Won't change as more people take the assessment.

Q. Can you retake the exam?
A. If you don't earn a skill badge for a given skill, you can retake the exam once more within six months. You can always delete your score and report if you feel the need. You won't be able to retrieve your report or recover your badge once you delete them. You also won't be able to retake the same assessment for three months

Q: How taking the assessment helps?
A. It's not mandatory for you to take the assessment. However, taking the assessment will help you stand out by showcasing that you have the desired skills of an ideal candidate, as well as increase your chances of getting noticed by other recruiters.
You may receive a link to the assessment because the recruiter for the job you've applied to has listed a skill as a

Desired Skill.
If you pass the assessment, recruiters will see the badge on your profile, if you choose to display it.
Recruiters won't be able to see your score.

CHAPTER II

List of available skill assessments on LinkedIn presently

Assessments available for technical skills:

- .NET Framework
- Agile Methodologies
- Amazon Web Services (AWS)
- Android
- AngularJS
- ArcGIS
- AWS
- AWS Lambda
- Bash
- C
- C#
- C++
- CSS
- Django
- Dreamweaver
- Eclipse
- Git
- Google Analytics
- Google Cloud Platform (GCP)
- Hadoop
- HTML
- Java
- JavaScript
- JQuery
- JSON
- Kotlin
- Machine Learning
- MATLAB
- Maven
- Microsoft Azure
- Microsoft T-SQL
- MongoDB
- MySQL
- Node.js
- NoSQL
- Objective-C
- Object-Oriented Programming
- PHP
- Python
- R Programming
- React.JS

- REST API
- Rhino 3D
- Ruby-on-Rails
- Scala
- Search Engine Optimization (SEO)
- Spring Framework
- Swift
- Unity
- Visual Basic for Applications (VBA)
- Windows Server
- WordPress
- XML

Assessments available for business skills:

- Adobe Acrobat
- Google Ads
- Microsoft Access
- Microsoft Excel
- Microsoft Outlook
- Microsoft Power Automate (Flow)
- Microsoft Power BI
- Microsoft PowerPoint
- Microsoft Project
- Microsoft SharePoint
- Microsoft Visio
- Microsoft Word
- QuickBooks

Assessments available for design skills:

- Adobe Animate
- Adobe Illustrator
- Adobe Lightroom
- Adobe Photoshop
- Adobe Premier Pro
- Adobe XD
- After Effects
- AutoCAD
- Autodesk Fusion 360
- Autodesk Inventor
- Autodesk Maya
- Avid Media Composer
- Final Cut Pro
- iMovie
- InDesign
- Keynote
- Logic Pro

- Pro Tools
- Revit
- SketchUp
- SOLIDWORKS

CHAPTER III

LinkedIn Skill Assessments Python (Programming Language)

Q1. What is an abstract class?
(a) An abstract class is the name for any class from which you can instantiate an object.
(b) Abstract classes must be redefined any time an object is instantiated from them.
(c) Abstract classes must inherit from concrete classes.
(d) An abstract class exists only so that other "concrete" classes can inherit from the abstract class.
Ans. (d)

Q2. What happens when you use the build-in function any() on a list?
(a) The any() function will randomly return any item from the list.
(b) The any() function returns True if any item in the list evaluates to True. Otherwise, it returns False.
(c) The any() function takes as arguments the list to check inside, and the item to check for. If "any" of the items in the list match the item to check for, the function returns True.
(d) The any() function returns a Boolean value that answers the question "Are there any items in this list?"
Ans. (b)

Q3. What data structure does a binary tree degenerate to if it isn't balanced properly?
(a) linked list
(b) queue
(c) set
(d) OrderedDict
Ans. (a)

Q4. What statement about static methods is true?
(a) Static methods are called static because they always return None.
(b) Static methods can be bound to either a class or an instance of a class.
(c) Static methods serve mostly as utility methods or helper methods, since they can't access or modify a class's state.
(d) Static methods can access and modify the state of a class or an instance of a class.
Ans. (c)

Q5. What are attributes?
(a) Attributes are long-form version of an if/else statement, used when testing for equality between objects.
(b) Attributes are a way to hold data or describe a state for a class or an instance of a class.
(c) Attributes are strings that describe characteristics of a class.
(d) Function arguments are called "attributes" in the context of class methods and instance methods.
Ans. (b)

Q6. What is the term to describe this code?
count, fruit, price = (2, 'apple', 3.5)
(a) tuple assignment
(b) tuple unpacking
(c) tuple matching
(d) tuple duplication

Ans. (b)

Q7. What built-in list method would you use to remove items from a list?
(a) .delete() method
(b) pop(my_list)
(c) del(my_list)
(d) .pop() method
Ans. (d)

Q8. What is one of the most common use of Python's sys library?
(a) to capture command-line arguments given at a file's runtime
(b) to connect various systems, such as connecting a web front end, an API service, a database, and a mobile app
(c) to take a snapshot of all the packages and libraries in your virtual environment
(d) to scan the health of your Python ecosystem while inside a virtual environment
Ans. (a)

Q9. What is the runtime of accessing a value in a dictionary by using its key?
(a) O(n), also called linear time.
(b) O(log n), also called logarithmic time.
(c) O(n^2), also called quadratic time.
(d) O(1), also called constant time.
Ans. (d)

Q10. Suppose you have a string variable defined as y="stuff;thing;junk;". What would be the output from this code?

```
Z = y.split(';')
len(z)
```

(a) 17
(b) 4
(c) 0
(d) 3
Ans. (b)

Q11. What is the correct way to write a doctest?

(a)

```
def sum(a, b):
""""
sum(4, 3)
7

sum(-4, 5)
1
""""
return a + b
```

(b)

```
def sum(a, b):
""""
>>> sum(4, 3)
7
```

```
>>> sum(-4, 5)
1
"""
return a + b
```

(c)

```
def sum(a, b):
"""
# >>> sum(4, 3)
# 7
# >>> sum(-4, 5)
# 1
"""
return a + b
```

(d)

```
def sum(a, b):
###
>>> sum(4, 3)
7
>>> sum(-4, 5)
1
###
return a + b
```

Ans. (b)

Q12. What built-in Python data type is commonly used to represent a stack?

(a) set
(b) list
(c) None
(d) dictionary
Ans. (b)

Q13. What would this expression return?

```
college_years = ['Freshman', 'Sophomore', 'Junior', 'Senior']
return list(enumerate(college_years, 2019))
```

(a) [('Freshman', 2019), ('Sophomore', 2020), ('Junior', 2021), ('Senior', 2022)]
(b) [(2019, 2020, 2021, 2022), ('Freshman', 'Sophomore', 'Junior', 'Senior')]
(c) [('Freshman', 'Sophomore', 'Junior', 'Senior'), (2019, 2020, 2021, 2022)]
(d) [(2019, 'Freshman'), (2020, 'Sophomore'), (2021, 'Junior'), (2022, 'Senior')]
Ans. (d)

Q14. How does defaultdict work?

(a) defaultdict will automatically create a dictionary for you that has keys which are the integers 0-10.
(b) defaultdict forces a dictionary to only accept keys that are of the types specified when you created the defaultdict (such as string or integers).
(c) If you try to access a key in a dictionary that doesn't exist, defaultdict will create a new key for you instead of throwing a KeyError.
(d) defaultdict stores a copy of a dictionary in memory that you can default to if the original gets unintentionally modified.

Ans. (c)

Q15. What is the correct syntax for defining a class called "Game", if it inherits from a parent class called "LogicGame"?

(a) class Game.LogicGame(): pass
(b) def Game(LogicGame): pass
(c) class Game(LogicGame): pass
(d) def Game.LogicGame(): pass
Ans. (c)

Q16. What is the purpose of the "self" keyword when defining or calling instance methods?

(a) self means that no other arguments are required to be passed into the method.
(b) There is no real purpose for the self method; it's just historic computer science jargon that Python keeps to stay consistent with other programming languages.
(c) self refers to the instance whose method was called.
(d) self refers to the class that was inherited from to create the object using self.
Ans. (c)

Q17. Which of these is NOT a characteristic of namedtuples?

(a) You can assign a name to each of the namedtuple members and refer to them that way, similarly to how you would access keys in dictionary.
(b) Each member of a namedtuple object can be indexed to directly, just like in a regular tuple.
(c) namedtuples are just as memory efficient as regular tuples.
(d) No import is needed to use namedtuples because they are available in the standard library.
Ans. (d)

Q18. What is an instance method?

(a) Instance methods can modify the state of an instance or the state of its parent class.
(b) Instance methods hold data related to the instance.
(c) An instance method is any class method that doesn't take any arguments.
(d) An instance method is a regular function that belongs to a class, but it must return None.
Ans. (a)

Q19. Which choice is the most syntactically correct example of the conditional branching?

(a)

```
num_people = 5
if num_people > 10:
print("There is a lot of people in the pool.")
elif num_people > 4;
print("There are some people in the pool.")
elif num_people > 0;
print("There are a few people in the pool.")
else:
print("There is no one in the pool.")
```

(b)

```
num_people = 5
if num_people > 10:
print("There is a lot of people in the pool.")
```

```
if num_people > 4:
print("There are some people in the pool.")
if num_people > 0:
print("There are a few people in the pool.")
else:
print("There is no one in the pool.")
```

(c)

```
num_people = 5
if num_people > 10:
    print("There is a lot of people in the pool.")
    elif num_people > 4:
    print("There are some people in the pool.")
    elif num_people > 0:
    print("There are a few people in the pool.")
    else:
    print("There is no one in the pool.")
```

(d)

```
    if num_people > 10;
    print("There is a lot of people in the pool.")
    if num_people > 4:
    print("There are some people in the pool.")
    if num_people > 0:
    print("There are a few people in the pool.")
    else:
    print("There is no one in the pool.")
```

Ans. (c)

Q20. Which statement does NOT describe the object-oriented programming concept of encapsulation?
(a) It protects the data from outside interference.
(b) A parent class is encapsulated and no data from the parent class passes on to the child class.
(c) It keeps data and the methods that can manipulate that data in one place.
(d) It only allows the data to be changed by methods.
Ans. (d)

Q21. What is the purpose of an if/else statement?
(a) It tells the computer which chunk of code to run if the instructions you coded are incorrect.
(b) It runs one chunk of code if all the imports were successful, and another chunk of code if the imports were not successful.
(c) It executes one chunk of code if a condition is true, but a different chunk of code if the condition is false.
(d) It tells the computer which chunk of code to run if the is enough memory to handle it, and which chunk of code to run if there is not enough memory to handle it.
Ans. (c)

Q22. What built-in Python data type is best suited for implementing a queue?
(a) dictionary
(b) set
(c) None. You can only build a queue from scratch.
(d) list

Ans. (d)

Q23. What is the correct syntax for instantiating a new object of the type Game?
(a) `my_game = class.Game()`
(b) `my_game = class(Game)`
(c) `my_game = Game()`
(d) `my_game = Game.create()`
Ans. (c)

Q24. What does the built-in `map()` function do?
(a) It creates a path from multiple values in an iterable to a single value.
(b) It applies a function to each item in an iterable and returns the value of that function.
(c) It converts a complex value type into simpler value types.
(d) It creates a mapping between two different elements of different iterables.
Ans. (b)

Q25. If you don't explicitly return a value from a function, what happens?
(a) The function will return a RuntimeError if you don't return a value.
(b) If the return keyword is absent, the function will return `None`.
(c) If the return keyword is absent, the function will return `True`.
(d) The function will enter an infinite loop because it won't know when to stop executing its code.
Ans. (b)

Q26. What is the purpose of the `pass` statement in Python?
(a) It is used to skip the `yield` statement of a generator and return a value of None.
(b) It is a null operation used mainly as a placeholder in functions, classes, etc.
(c) It is used to pass control from one statement block to another.
(d) It is used to skip the rest of a `while` or `for loop` and return to the start of the loop.
Ans. (b)

Q27. What is the term used to describe items that may be passed into a function?
(a) arguments
(b) paradigms
(c) attributes
(d) decorators
Ans. (a)

Q28. Which collection type is used to associate values with unique keys?
(a) `slot`
(b) `dictionary`
(c) `queue`
(d) `sorted list`
Ans. (b)

Q29. When does a for loop stop iterating?
(a) when it encounters an infinite loop
(b) when it encounters an if/else statement that contains a break keyword
(c) when it has assessed each item in the iterable it is working on or a break keyword is encountered

(d) when the runtime for the loop exceeds O(n^2)
Ans. (c)

Q30. Assuming the node is in a singly linked list, what is the runtime complexity of searching for a specific node within a singly linked list?

(a) The runtime is O(n) because in the worst case, the node you are searching for is the last node, and every node in the linked list must be visited.
(b) The runtime is O(nk), with n representing the number of nodes and k representing the amount of time it takes to access each node in memory.
(c) The runtime cannot be determined unless you know how many nodes are in the singly linked list.
(d) The runtime is O(1) because you can index directly to a node in a singly linked list.
Ans. (a)

Q31. Given the following three list, how would you create a new list that matches the desired output printed below?

```
fruits = ['Apples', 'Oranges', 'Bananas']
quantities = [5, 3, 4]
prices = [1.50, 2.25, 0.89]
#Desired output
[('Apples', 5, 1.50),
('Oranges', 3, 2.25),
('Bananas', 4, 0.89)]
```

(a)

```
output = []
fruit_tuple_0 = (first[0], quantities[0], price[0])
output.append(fruit_tuple)
fruit_tuple_1 = (first[1], quantities[1], price[1])
output.append(fruit_tuple)
fruit_tuple_2 = (first[2], quantities[2], price[2])
output.append(fruit_tuple)
return output
```

(b)

```
i = 0
output = []
for fruit in fruits:
temp_qty = quantities[i]
temp_price = prices[i]
output.append((fruit, temp_qty, temp_price))
i += 1
return output
```

(c)

```
groceries = zip(fruits, quantities, prices)
return groceries
>>> [
('Apples', 5, 1.50),
('Oranges', 3, 2.25),
('Bananas', 4, 0.89)
```

]

(d)

```
i = 0
output = []
for fruit in fruits:
for qty in quantities:
for price in prices:
output.append((fruit, qty, price))
i += 1
return output
```

Ans. (b)

Q32. What happens when you use the built-in function all() on a list?

(a) The `all()` function returns a Boolean value that answers the question "Are all the items in this list the same?

(b) The `all()` function returns True if all the items in the list can be converted to strings. Otherwise, it returns False.

(c) The `all()` function will return all the values in the list.

(d) The `all()` function returns True if all items in the list evaluate to True. Otherwise, it returns False.

Ans. (d)

Q33. What is the correct syntax for calling an instance method on a class named Game?

(a)

```
>>> dice = Game()
>>> dice.roll()
```

(b)

```
>>> dice = Game(self)
>>> dice.roll(self)
```

(c)

```
>>> dice = Game()
>>> dice.roll(self)
```

(d)

```
>>> dice = Game(self)
>>> dice.roll()
```

Ans. (a)

Q34. What is the algorithmic paradigm of quick sort?

(a) backtracking

(b) dynamic programming

(c) decrease and conquer

(d) divide and conquer

Ans. (d)

Q35. What is runtime complexity of the list's built-in `.append()` method?

(a) O(1), also called constant time

(b) O(log n), also called logarithmic time

(c) O(n^2), also called quadratic time

(d) O(n), also called linear time

Ans. (a)

Q36. What is key difference between a `set` and a `list`?

(a) A set is an ordered collection unique items. A list is an unordered collection of non-unique items.
(b) Elements can be retrieved from a list but they cannot be retrieved from a set.
(c) A set is an ordered collection of non-unique items. A list is an unordered collection of unique items.
(d) A set is an unordered collection unique items. A list is an ordered collection of non-unique items.
Ans. (d)

Q37. What is the definition of abstraction as applied to object-oriented Python?

(a) Abstraction means that a different style of code can be used, since many details are already known to the program behind the scenes.
(b) Abstraction means the implementation is hidden from the user, and only the relevant data or information is shown.
(c) Abstraction means that the data and the functionality of a class are combined into one entity.
(d) Abstraction means that a class can inherit from more than one parent class.
Ans. (b)

Q38. What does this function print?

```
def print_alpha_nums(abc_list, num_list):
    for char in abc_list:
    for num in num_list:
    print(char, num)
    return
print_alpha_nums(['a', 'b', 'c'], [1, 2, 3])
```

(a)

```
a 1
a 2
a 3
b 1
b 2
b 3
c 1
c 2
c 3
```

(b)

```
['a', 'b', 'c'], [1, 2, 3]
```

(c)

```
aaa
bbb
ccc
111
222
333
```

(d)

```
a 1 2 3
b 1 2 3
c 1 2 3
```

Ans. (a)

Q39. Correct representation of doctest for function in Python

(a)
```
def sum(a, b):
# a = 1
# b = 2
# sum(a, b) = 3
return a + b
```
(b)
```
def sum(a, b):
"""
a = 1
b = 2
sum(a, b) = 3
"""
return a + b
```
(c)
```
def sum(a, b):
"""
>>> a = 1
>>> b = 2
>>> sum(a, b)
3
"""
return a + b
```
(d)
```
def sum(a, b):
‘’’
a = 1
b = 2
sum(a, b) = 3
‘’’
return a + b
```
Ans. (c)

Q40. Suppose a Game class inherits from two parent classes: BoardGame and LogicGame. Which statement is true about the methods of an object instantiated from the Game class?

(a) When instantiating an object, the object doesn’t inherit any of the parent class’s methods.
(b) When instantiating an object, the object will inherit the methods of whichever parent class has more methods.
(c) When instantiating an object, the programmer must specify which parent class to inherit methods from.
(d) An instance of the Game class will inherit whatever methods the BoardGame and LogicGame classes have.
Ans. (d)

Q41. What does calling namedtuple on a collection type return?

(a) a generic object class with iterable parameter fields
(b) a generic object class with non-iterable named fields
(c) a tuple subclass with non-iterable parameter fields
(d) a tuple subclass with iterable named fields

Ans. (d)

Q42. What symbol(s) do you use to assess equality between two elements?
(a) `&&`
(b) `=`
(c) `==`
(d) `||`
Ans. (c)

Q43. Review the code below. What is the correct syntax for changing the price to 1.5?
fruit_info = {
'fruit': 'apple',
'count': 2,
'price': 3.5
}
(a) `fruit_info ['price'] = 1.5`
(b) `my_list [3.5] = 1.5`
(c) `1.5 = fruit_info ['price]`
(d) `my_list['price'] == 1.5`
Ans. (a)

Q44. What value would be returned by this check for equality?
5 != 6
(a) `yes`
(b) `False`
(c) `True`
(d) `None`
Ans. (c)

Q45. What does a class's `init()` method do?
(a) The `__init__` method makes classes aware of each other if more than one class is defined in a single code file.
(b) The`__init__` method is included to preserve backwards compatibility from Python 3 to Python 2, but no longer needs to be used in Python 3.
(c) The `__init__` method is a constructor method that is called automatically whenever a new object is created from a class. It sets the initial state of a new object.
(d) The `__init__` method initializes any imports you may have included at the top of your file.
Ans. (c)

Q46. What is meant by the phrase "space complexity"?
(a) `How many microprocessors it would take to run your code in less than one second`
(b) `How many lines of code are in your code file`
(c) `The amount of space taken up in memory as a function of the input size`
(d) `How many copies of the code file could fit in 1 GB of memory`
Ans. (c)

Q47. What is the correct syntax for creating a variable that is bound to a dictionary?

(a) `fruit_info = {'fruit': 'apple', 'count': 2, 'price': 3.5}`
(b) `fruit_info =('fruit': 'apple', 'count': 2,'price': 3.5 ).dict()`
(c) `fruit_info = ['fruit': 'apple', 'count': 2,'price': 3.5 ].dict()`
(d) `fruit_info = to_dict('fruit': 'apple', 'count': 2, 'price': 3.5)`
Ans. (a)

Q48. What is the proper way to write a list comprehension that represents all the keys in this dictionary?
`fruits = {'Apples': 5, 'Oranges': 3, 'Bananas': 4}`
(a) `fruit_names = [x in fruits.keys() for x]`
(b) `fruit_names = for x in fruits.keys() *``fruit_names = for x in fruits.keys() *`
(c) `fruit_names = [x for x in fruits.keys()]`
(d) `fruit_names = x for x in fruits.keys()`
Ans. (c)

Q49. What is the purpose of the `self` keyword when defining or calling methods on an instance of an object?
(a) `self` refers to the class that was inherited from to create the object using `self`.
(b) There is no real purpose for the `self` method. It's just legacy computer science jargon that Python keeps to stay consistent with other programming languages.
(c) `self` means that no other arguments are required to be passed into the method.
(d) `self` refers to the instance whose method was called.
Ans. (d)

Q50. What statement about the class methods is true?
(a) A class method is a regular function that belongs to a class, but it must return None.
(b) A class method can modify the state of the class, but they can't directly modify the state of an instance that inherits from that class.
(c) A class method is similar to a regular function, but a class method doesn't take any arguments.
(d) A class method hold all of the data for a particular class.
Ans. (b)

Q51. What does it mean for a function to have linear runtime?
(a) You did not use very many advanced computer programming concepts in your code.
(b) The difficulty level your code is written at is not that high.
(c) It will take your program less than half a second to run.
(d) The amount of time it takes the function to complete grows linearly as the input size increases.
Ans. (d)

Q52. What is the proper way to define a function?
(a) `def getMaxNum(list_of_nums): # body of function goes here`
(b) `func get_max_num(list_of_nums): # body of function goes here`
(c) `func getMaxNum(list_of_nums): # body of function goes here`
(d) `def get_max_num(list_of_nums): # body of function goes here`
Ans. (d)

Q53. According to the PEP 8 coding style guidelines, how should constant values be named in Python?
(a) in camel case without using underscores to separate words -- e.g. `maxValue = 255`
(b) in lowercase with underscores to separate words -- e.g. `max_value = 255`
(c) in all caps with underscores separating words -- e.g. `MAX_VALUE = 255`

(d) in mixed case without using underscores to separate words -- e.g. `MaxValue = 255`
Ans. (c)

Q54. Describe the functionality of a deque.
(a) A deque adds items to one side and remove items from the other side.
(b) A deque adds items to either or both sides, but only removes items from the top.
(c) A deque adds items at either or both ends, and remove items at either or both ends.
(d) A deque adds items only to the top, but remove from either or both sides.
Ans. (c)

Q55. What is the correct syntax for creating a variable that is bound to a set?
(a) my_set = {0, 'apple', 3.5}
(b) my_set = to_set(0, 'apple', 3.5)
(c) my_set = (0, 'apple', 3.5).to_set()
(d) my_set = (0, 'apple', 3.5).set()
Ans. (a)

Q56. What is the correct syntax for defining an __init__() method that takes no parameters?
(a)
```
class __init__(self):
pass
```
(b)
```
def __init__():
pass
```
(c)
```
class __init__():
pass
```
(d)
```
def __init__(self):
pass
```
Ans. (d)

Q57. Which of the following is TRUE About how numeric data would be organised in a binary Search tree?
(a) For any given Node in a binary Search Tree, the child node to the left is less than the value of the given node and the child node to its right is greater than the given node.
(b) Binary Search Tree cannot be used to organize and search through numeric data, given the complication that arise with very deep trees.
(c) The top node of the binary search tree would be an arbitrary number. All the nodes to the left of the top node need to be less than the top node's number, but they don't need to ordered in any particular way.
(d) The smallest numeric value would go in the top most node. The next highest number would go in its left child node, the the next highest number after that would go in its right child node. This pattern would continue until all numeric values were in their own node.
Ans. (a)

Q58. Why would you use a decorator?
(a) A decorator is similar to a class and should be used if you are doing functional programming instead of object oriented programming.
(b) A decorator is a visual indicator to someone reading your code that a portion of your code is critical and should

not be changed.
(c) You use the decorator to alter the functionality of a function without having to modify the functions code.
(d) An import statement is preceded by a decorator, python knows to import the most recent version of whatever package or library is being imported.
Ans. (c)

Q59. When would you use a for loop?
(a) Only in some situations, as loops are used only for certain type of programming.
(b) When you need to check every element in an iterable of known length.
(c) When you want to minimize the use of strings in your code.
(d) When you want to run code in one file for a function in another file.
Ans. (b)

Q60. What is the most self-descriptive way to define a function that calculates sales tax on a purchase?
(a)
def tax(my_float):
"'Calculates the sales tax of a purchase. Takes in a float representing the subtotal as an argument and returns a float representing the sales tax."'
pass
(b)
def tx(amt):
"'Gets the tax on an amount."'
(c)
def sales_tax(amount):
"'Calculates the sales tax of a purchase. Takes in a float representing the subtotal as an argument and returns a float representing the sales tax."'
(d)
def calculate_sales_tax(subtotal):
pass
Ans. (d)

Q61. What would happen if you did not alter the state of the element that an algorithm is operating on recursively?
(a) You do not have to alter the state of the element the algorithm is recursing on.
(b) You would eventually get a KeyError when the recursive portion of the code ran out of items to recurse on.
(c) You would get a RuntimeError: maximum recursion depth exceeded.
(d) The function using recursion would return None.
Ans. (c)

Q62. What is the runtime complexity of searching for an item in a binary search tree?
(a) The runtime for searching in a binary search tree is O(1) because each node acts as a key, similar to a dictionary.
(b) The runtime for searching in a binary search tree is O(n!) because every node must be compared to every other node.
(c) The runtime for searching in a binary search tree is generally O(h), where h is the height of the tree.
(d) The runtime for searching in a binary search tree is O(n) because every node in the tree must be visited.
Ans. (c)

Q63. Why would you use `mixin`?

(a) You use a `mixin` to force a function to accept an argument at runtime even if the argument wasn't included in the function's definition.
(b) You use a `mixin` to allow a decorator to accept keyword arguments.
(c) You use a `mixin` to make sure that a class's attributes and methods don't interfere with global variables and functions.
(d) If you have many classes that all need to have the same functionality, you'd use a `mixin` to define that functionality.
Ans. (d)

Q64. What is the runtime complexity of adding an item to a stack and removing an item from a stack?
(a) Add items to a stack in O(1) time and remove items from a stack on O(n) time.
(b) Add items to a stack in O(1) time and remove items from a stack in O(1) time.
(c) Add items to a stack in O(n) time and remove items from a stack on O(1) time.
(d) Add items to a stack in O(n) time and remove items from a stack on O(n) time.
Ans. (b)

Q65. Which statement accurately describes how items are added to and removed from a stack?
(a) a stack adds items to one side and removes items from the other side.
(b) a stack adds items to the top and removes items from the top.
(c) a stack adds items to the top and removes items from anywhere in the stack.
(d) a stack adds items to either end and removes items from either end.
Ans. (b)

Q66. What is a base case in a recursive function?
(a) A base case is the condition that allows the algorithm to stop recursing. It is usually a problem that is small enough to solve directly.
(b) The base case is summary of the overall problem that needs to be solved.
(c) The base case is passed in as an argument to a function whose body makes use of recursion.
(d) The base case is similar to a base class, in that it can be inherited by another object.
Ans. (a)

Q67. Why is it considered good practice to open a file from within a Python script by using the `with` keyword?
(a) The `with` keyword lets you choose which application to open the file in.
(b) The `with` keyword acts like a `for` loop, and lets you access each line in the file one by one.
(c) There is no benefit to using the `with` keyword for opening a file in Python.
(d) When you open a file using the `with` keyword in Python, Python will make sure the file gets closed, even if an exception or error is thrown.
Ans. (d)

Q68. Why would you use a virtual environment?
(a) Virtual environments create a "bubble" around your project so that any libraries or packages you install within it don't affect your entire machine.
(b) Teams with remote employees use virtual environments so they can share code, do code reviews, and collaborate remotely.
(c) Virtual environments were common in Python 2 because they augmented missing features in the language. Virtual environments are not necessary in Python 3 due to advancements in the language.
(d) Virtual environments are tied to your GitHub or Bitbucket account, allowing you to access any of your repos virtually from any machine.

Ans. (a)

Q69. What is the correct way to run all the doctests in a given file from the command line?
(a) python3 -m doctest <_filename_>
(b) python3 <_filename_>
(c) python3 <_filename_> rundoctests
(d) python3 doctest
Ans. (a)

Q70. What is a lambda function ?
(a) any function that makes use of scientific or mathematical constants, often represented by Greek letters in academic writing
(b) a function that get executed when decorators are used
(c) any function whose definition is contained within five lines of code or fewer
(d) a small, anonymous function that can take any number of arguments but has only expression to evaluate
Ans. (d)

Q71. What is the primary difference between lists and tuples?
(a) You can access a specifc element in a list by indexing to its position, but you cannot access a specific element in a tuple unless you iterate through the tuple
(b) Lists are mutable, meaning you can change the data that is inside them at any time. Tuples are immutable, meaning you cannot change the data that is inside them once you have created the tuple.
(c) Lists are immutable, meaning you cannot change the data that is inside them once you have created the list. Tuples are mutable, meaning you can change the data that is inside them at any time.
(d) Lists can hold several data types inside them at once, but tuples can only hold the same data type if multiple elements are present.
Ans. (b)

Q72. Which statement about static method is true?
(a) Static methods can be bound to either a class or an instance of a class.
(b) Static methods can access and modify the state of a class or an instance of a class.
(c) Static methods serve mostly as utility or helper methods, since they cannot access or modify a class's state.
(d) Static methods are called static because they always return None.
Ans. (c)

Q73. What does a generator return?
(a) None
(b) An iterable object
(c) A linked list data structure from a non-empty list
(d) All the keys of the given dictionary
Ans. (b)

Q74. What is the difference between class attributes and instance attributes?
(a) Instance attributes can be changed, but class attributes cannot be changed
(b) Class attributes are shared by all instances of the class. Instance attributes may be unique to just that instance
(c) There is no difference between class attributes and instance attributes
(d) Class attributes belong just to the class, not to instance of that class. Instance attributes are shared among all instances of a class

Ans. (b)

Q75. What is the correct syntax of creating an instance method?

(a)
```
def get_next_card():
# method body goes here
```
(b)
```
def get_next_card(self):
# method body goes here
```
(c)
```
def self.get_next_card():
# method body goes here
```
(d)
```
def self.get_next_card(self):
# method body goes here
```
Ans. (d)

Q76. What is the correct way to call a function?

(a) get_max_num([57, 99, 31, 18])
(b) call.(get_max_num)
(c) def get_max_num([57, 99, 31, 18])
(d) call.get_max_num([57, 99, 31, 18])
Ans. (a)

Q77. How is comment created?

(a) -- This is a comment
(b) # This is a comment
(c) /_ This is a comment _\
(d) // This is a comment
Ans. (b)

Q78. What is the correct syntax for replacing the string apple in the list with the string orange?

(a) orange = my_list[1]
(b) my_list[1] = 'orange'
(c) my_list['orange'] = 1
(d) my_list[1] == orange
Ans. (b)

Q79. What will happen if you use a while loop and forget to include logic that eventually causes the while loop to stop?

(a) Nothing will happen; your computer knows when to stop running the code in the while loop.
(b) You will get a KeyError.
(c) Your code will get stuck in an infinite loop.
(d) You will get a WhileLoopError.
Ans. (c)

Q80. Describe the functionality of a queue?

(a) A queue adds items to either end and removes items from either end.
(b) A queue adds items to the top and removes items from the top.
(c) A queue adds items to the top, and removes items from anywhere in, a list.
(d) A queue adds items to the top and removes items from anywhere in the queue.
Ans. (a)

Q81. Which choice is the most syntactically correct example of the conditional branching?
(a)
```
num_people = 5
if num_people > 10:
print("There is a lot of people in the pool.")
elif num_people > 4:
print("There are some people in the pool.")
else:
print("There is no one in the pool.")
```
(b)
```
num_people = 5
if num_people > 10:
print("There is a lot of people in the pool.")
if num_people > 4:
print("There are some people in the pool.")
else:
print("There is no one in the pool.")
```
(c)
```
num_people = 5

if num_people > 10;
print("There is a lot of people in the pool.")
elif num_people > 4;
print("There are some people in the pool.")
else;
print("There is no one in the pool.")
```
(d)
```
if num_people > 10;
print("There is a lot of people in the pool.")
if num_people > 4;
print("There are some people in the pool.")
else;
print("There is no one in the pool.")
```
Ans. (a)

Q82. How does `defaultdict` work?
(a) `defaultdict` will automatically create a dictionary for you that has keys which are the integers 0-10.
(b) `defaultdict` forces a dictionary to only accept keys that are of the types specified when you created the `defaultdict` (such as strings or integers).
(c) If you try to read from a `defaultdict` with a nonexistent key, a new default key-value pair will be created for you instead of throwing a `KeyError`.
(d) `defaultdict` stores a copy of a dictionary in memory that you can default to if the original gets unintentionally

modified.
Ans. (c)

Q83. What is the correct syntax for adding a key called `variety` to the `fruit_info` dictionary that has a value of `Red Delicious`?
(a) `fruit_info['variety'] == 'Red Delicious'`
(b) `fruit_info['variety'] = 'Red Delicious'`
(c) `red_delicious = fruit_info['variety']`
(d) `red_delicious == fruit_info['variety']`
Ans. (b)

Q84. When would you use a `while` loop?
(a) when you want to minimize the use of strings in your code
(b) when you want to run code in one file while code in another file is also running
(c) when you want some code to continue running as long as some condition is true
(d) when you need to run two or more chunks of code at once within the same file
Ans. (c)

Q85. What is the correct syntax for defining an `__init__()` method that sets instance-specific attributes upon creation of a new class instance?
(a)
```
def __init__(self, attr1, attr2):
attr1 = attr1
attr2 = attr2
```
(b)
```
def __init__(attr1, attr2):
attr1 = attr1
attr2 = attr2
```
(c)
```
def __init__(self, attr1, attr2):
self.attr1 = attr1
self.attr2 = attr2
```
(d)
```
def __init__(attr1, attr2):
self.attr1 = attr1
self.attr2 = attr2
```
Ans. (c)

Q86. What would this recursive function print if it is called with no parameters?
```
def count_recursive(n=1):
if n > 3:
return
print(n)
count_recursive(n + 1)
```
(a)
1
1
2

2
3
3
(b)
3
2
1
(c)
3
3
2
2
1
1
(d)
1
2
3
Ans. (d)

Q87. In Python, when using sets, you use ___ to calculate the intersection between two sets and ___ to calculate the union.
(a) Intersect;union
(b) |; &
(c) &; |
(d) &&; ||
Ans. (c)

Q88. What will this code fragment return?
import numpy as np
np.ones([1,2,3,4,5])
(a) It returns a 5x5 matric; each row will have the values 1,2,3,4,5.
(b) It returns an array with the values 1,2,3,4,5
(c) It returns five different square matrices filled with ones. The first is 1x1, the second 2x2, and so on to 5x5
(d) It returns a 5-dimensional array of size 1x2x3x4x5 filled with 1s.
Ans. (d)

Q89. You encounter a FileNotFoundException while using just the filename in the open function. What might be the easiest solution?
(a) Make sure the file is on the system PATH
(b) Create a symbolic link to allow better access to the file
(c) Copy the file to the same directory as where the script is running from
(d) Add the path to the file to the PYTHONPATH environment variable
Ans. (c)

Q90. what will this command return?
{x for x in range(100) if x%3 == 0}
(a) a set of all the multiples of 3 less then 100

(b) a set of all the number from 0 to 100 multiplied by 3
(c) a list of all the multiples of 3 less then 100
(d) a set of all the multiples of 3 less then 100 excluding 0
Ans. (a)

Q91. What does the // operator in Python 3 allow you to do?
(a) Perform integer division
(b) Perform operations on exponents
(c) Find the remainder of a division operation
(d) Perform floating point division
Ans. (a)

Q92. This code provides the _____ of the list of numbers
num_list =[21,13,19,3,11,5,18]
num_list.sort()
num_list[len(num_list)//2]
(a) mean
(b) mode
(c) median
(d) average
Ans. (c)

Q93. Which statement about the class methods is true?
(a) A class method holds all of the data for a particular class.
(b) A class method can modify the state of the class, but it cannot directly modify the state of an instance that inherits from that class.
(c) A class method is a regular function that belongs to a class, but it must return None
(d) A class method is similar to a regular function, but a class method does not take any arguments.
Ans. (b)

Q94. What file is imported to use dates in python?
(a) datetime
(b) dateday
(c) daytime
(d) timedate
Ans. (a)

Q95. What is the correct syntax for defining a class called Game?
(a) def Game(): pass
(b) def Game: pass
(c) class Game: pass
(d) class Game(): pass
Ans. (c)

Q96. What does a class's __init__() method do?
(a) The __init__ method makes classes aware of each other if more than one class is defined in a single code file.
(b) The __nit__ method is included to preserve backward compatibility from Python 3 to Python 2, but no longer needs to be used in Python 3.

(c) The __init__ method is a constructor method that is called automatically whenever a new object is created from a class. It sets the initial state of a new object.
(d) The __init__ method initializes any imports you may have included at the top of your file.
Ans. (c)

Q97. What is the correct syntax for calling an instance method on a class named Game?
(a) my_game = Game(self) self.my_game.roll_dice()
(b) my_game = Game() self.my_game.roll_dice()
(c) my_game = Game() my_game.roll_dice()
(d) my_game = Game(self) my_game.roll_dice(self)
Ans. (b)

Q98. What is the output of this code? (NumPy has been imported as np.)?
a = np.array([1,2,3,4])
print(a[[False, True, False, False]])
(a) {0,2}
(b) [2]
(c) {2}
(d) [0,2,0,0]
Ans. (b)

Your Feedback is Valued

Thank you for buying this book. Hope you liked it. This book is authored by a team of expert teachers, educators, trainers and tutors with several years of teaching experience. With the experience of coaching and mentoring thousands of students from CBSE, CISCE (ICSE or ISC), IGCSE and IB boards, the books have been written to help the students score maximum marks in their final board exams, term 1 and term 2 exams, mock tests, pre-boards, sample papers, prelims, school terms, unit tests, mid-terms, guess papers, term exams, school tests, chapter tests, topic tests as well as to complete any of the homework assignments, timed practice tests, worksheets, projects, quizzes etc. The teachers have been providing the best coaching for prestigious competitions including IIT-JEE and NEET competitive exams. The faculty have tried to shared the best practices gained from the experience of teaching school students, college students, Indian as well as international students. Having taught children according to the competency based education as well as constantly updating themselves with the latest National Education Policy (NEP) 2020, these books are planned so as to keep them updated as per the vision of India's new education system and latest curriculum changes.

You can find more such books by AV Editorial Board at Amazon: https://www.amazon.in/s?k=av+editorial+board

You can also search for "AV Editorial Board Books" at Amazon's website. https://www.amazon.in/

If this book met your expectations, please leave a review or give your rating for this book. In case you have any issues or suggestions regarding this book or want us to make some improvements, please send an email to aveditorialboard@gmail.comWe will try to make the necessary changes in the future versions/editions of this book. Thanks for your time.

9 798885 215817

Printed by Libri Plureos GmbH in Hamburg,
Germany